The Awesome Miss Seeds

Her Courage Overcame Disabilities;
Her Determination Changed Schools and Teaching

Dolores A. Escobar; Sandra R. Radoff

Illustrated by Stephen Adams

AuthorHouse™
1663 Liberty Drive
Bloomington, IN 47403
www.authorhouse.com
Phone: 1 (800) 839-8640

Published by AuthorHouse 09/12/2016

ISBN: 978-1-5049-7434-9 (sc)
978-1-5246-3883-2 (hc)
978-1-5049-7433-2 (e)

Library of Congress Control Number: 2016900979

Print information available on the last page.

Any people depicted in stock imagery provided by Thinkstock are models, and such images are being used for illustrative purposes only. Certain stock imagery © Thinkstock.

This book is printed on acid-free paper.

authorHOUSE®

This book is dedicated to all the children whose elementary school days became meaningful, relevant, and enjoyable because of Miss Seeds's dedication and determination.

By the time Corinne Seeds reached third grade she hated school!

While the teacher talked, Corinne wiggled and squirmed. She twisted and turned. She played with pencils and books on her desk. Sometimes she made noises.

"Corinne, look at me! Listen to me," the teacher scolded.

Corinne merely turned and frowned.

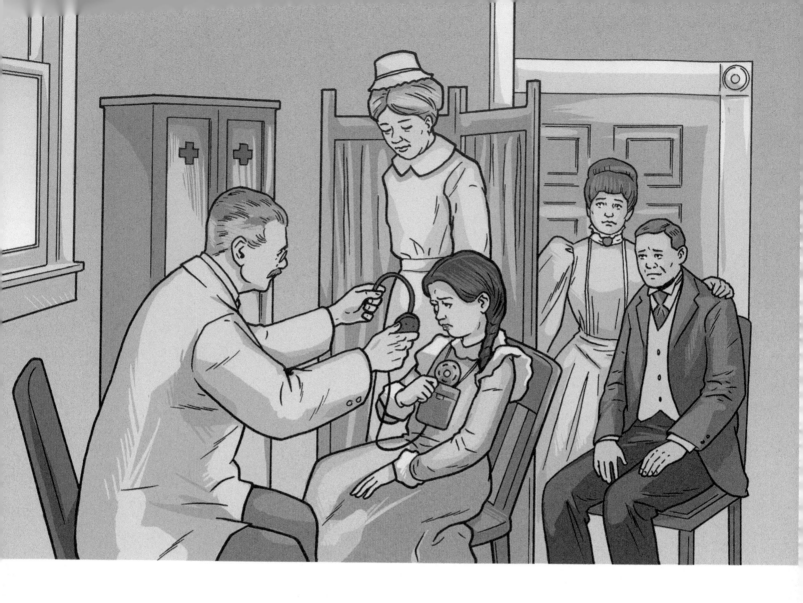

Eventually, the teacher met with Corinne's parents and told them, "Corinne does not listen. She does not follow directions. Instead of learning her lessons, she misbehaves."

Corinne's parents were surprised and worried. Something had to be wrong. At home, Corinne was well behaved. She was curious. She asked many questions. She had been eager to begin school, although lately she seldom talked about school.

Following their meeting with the third grade teacher, Corinne's parents took her to a doctor. After several tests, the doctor told them, "Corinne is almost deaf. *And* she has very poor eyesight. She can only see things very close to her. No wonder she doesn't pay attention in school. However, we can help her."

The doctor gave Corinne glasses with thick lenses and a hearing aid to help her hear sounds more clearly. All this happened a long time ago when hearing aids were big and bulky. The batteries for the hearing aid hung in a cardboard box under her blouse and rested on Corinne's chest. Wires from the batteries connected to earphones in her ears.

At first, Corinne found it difficult to adjust the hearing aid so that sounds were neither too loud nor too soft. When she struggled to adjust the hearing aid, she frowned. When she put on her thick glasses and struggled to see things in the distance, she frowned fiercely. Sometimes her frowns made people who didn't know her think she was unfriendly.

However, Corinne's hearing aid and glasses enabled her to do schoolwork easily. She became an excellent reader. While other children played outdoor games, Corinne read books. Books became her best friends. She especially loved to read stories about people who lived long ago or in faraway places.

One of Corinne's favorite pastimes was to play school. Of course, she was always the teacher; she read stories to her dolls or to younger children in the neighborhood.

As Corinne progressed from grade to grade at school, some teachers offered to help her learn her lessons. Corinne appreciated their help. Her own mother had been a teacher before Corinne was born and had taught Corinne to respect and appreciate teachers. Most important, Corinne realized that teachers did meaningful work when they helped her and other children learn. Corinne wanted to do something worthwhile with her life too; she began to think about becoming a teacher.

By the time Corinne graduated from high school, she was sure she wanted to teach. She entered a college that would prepare her to be a teacher. Some people in the school said Corinne should not teach because of her poor eyesight and hearing disability. Corinne was worried and asked her mother for advice.

"Are you going to let other people tell you what you can or cannot do?" her mother asked.

With a determined frown, Corinne answered, "No, I know I can be a good teacher. I *will* graduate!" And Corinne did graduate. Soon she became "Miss Seeds," an elementary schoolteacher.

When Miss Seeds faced her first class, fifty children sat in long rows of desks in chairs that did not move. This was the way elementary schoolrooms looked in Miss Seeds's day. If a boy or girl misbehaved, Miss Seeds could ask the principal to spank the child. Do you think she ever asked the principal to spank one of her students? No! Never! But she came close to it.

One day Miss Seeds entered her classroom and saw William standing on his desk, dancing and barking like a dog. The other children were laughing wildly. Miss Seeds took William off the desk, scolded him angrily, and then quieted the children.

Miss Seeds felt terrible and a bit sad too. She wanted to be a teacher who cared and respected every child, even William. She wanted her students to be more interested in their schoolwork than in William's foolishness. She thought, *How could I have helped William want to learn? Why was he acting silly? Was the class misbehaving because I haven't been a good teacher? How can I become a better teacher?*

To learn more about teaching and to do the work Miss Seeds considered very important, she took a job teaching grown-ups at a night school. Most of her students were immigrants—people new to America. They spoke different languages. Some were of different races. These students went to class after they finished their day jobs. Miss Seeds taught them to read and write English so they could become good citizens of the United States of America.

The night-school students told Miss Seeds about their homelands and customs. Miss Seeds not only loved their stories, but she also learned to respect and appreciate these hardworking people. The night-school students taught Miss Seeds important lessons about the ways in which people differed but also the ways in which people were alike. These lessons about people influenced Miss Seeds throughout the rest of her life.

Always eager to improve her teaching, Miss Seeds read many books. One day she read about a man who had new ideas about teaching and learning. His name was Dr. John Dewey. He believed that learning was a natural part of living and being active. He said, "Children learn best by doing, not by sitting and listening to the teacher." He believed schools should be places where children enjoyed learning because they were interested in their studies. He believed teachers were important, but children were important individuals too. Schools should be places, he said, where teachers and students practiced working together with respect for one another. This way of thinking about schools and teaching became known as *progressive education*.

Dewey's ideas excited Miss Seeds. She was unhappy with schools as she knew them. She felt his ideas could change the way children were taught and make schools places where children enjoyed learning. She had to know more. She decided to go to Columbia University in New York to study with Dr. Dewey.

"What? Travel alone from California to New York? Leave your family?" her parents asked her. Few young women in Miss Seeds's day traveled long distances alone. Nevertheless, Miss Seeds gave a determined frown and bravely made plans to leave.

Miss Seeds was accepted at Columbia University, but some folks in California wrote to the university, stating that Miss Seeds's disabilities would keep her from completing her studies. If she did complete her studies, they suggested, her disabilities would prevent her from being considered for higher positions. However, Miss Seeds was determined to prove them wrong!

When Miss Seeds saw Dr. Dewey's ideas in action, she was delighted. In his school, children were busy working on their projects. One group learned how plants grew by planting a garden, observing plant growth, and writing about the changes. Another group learned how airplanes flew by making model airplanes and flying them. Children created plays, danced, and painted pictures about their studies. Everywhere, children asked questions and read to find answers to *their* questions. This was a school where children enjoyed learning and were interested in their projects—no need for spankings here!

Miss Seeds had found her mission in life: she would spread Dr. Dewey's ideas. She would change the way teachers taught and change the very nature of schools.

When Miss Seeds returned to California, she wrote papers and gave talks to groups of educators and parents about why teachers must use these new, progressive ideas. She became known as a "progressive pioneer," a leader blazing new trails for teachers and children.

It wasn't surprising that when the University of California at Los Angeles (UCLA) created a training school for elementary schoolteachers on its campus, Miss Seeds was chosen as its principal. As principal of the University Elementary School (UES), Miss Seeds created her vision of a progressive school.

For the next thirty years, Miss Seeds led an experiment in progressive education at UES. She taught Dewey's ideas to teachers working in schools and to students studying to be teachers at UCLA. She and her teachers also created new ways to use Dewey's ideas. UES teachers wrote classroom guides for other teachers that reflected Miss Seeds's belief: children learn the most valuable lessons by studying the people of the world today, as well as those who lived long ago. UES became a showplace for teachers, principals, and parents. People came from near and far to listen, watch, and learn.

At UES on any given day, visitors would see children at work. Children might be using many types of tools, sewing or weaving to make items for `use in their play. A class might be using those items to enact a day in the lives of the Pilgrims, an afternoon in a Mexican marketplace, or a "fiesta" on a ranch during the early days of California.

Out on the playground children might be discussing the trails leading west to California and deciding which one the wagon train should take. At other times they might be panning for gold in a nearby stream, or planning to take a field trip to the foot hills where gold was found during the "gold rush."

Another class might be in a large room creatively moving their bodies with music to show how underwater grasses sway with the waves, how birds soar in flight, or how a 'toreador' might move to tease the bull during a bullfight. Still other children might be cooking, sewing, or weaving, depending on the people they were studying. Everywhere, children would be active, planning the next steps for their projects, solving problems, asking questions, and searching for answers.

Everywhere, teachers respectfully guided each and every child to be part of the activity, to participate, and to contribute to class projects.

Classrooms at UES were alive with paintings, stories, and items that the children created. Tables and chairs were movable, arranged for discussion and small-group work, or pushed aside for play or construction.

Miss Seeds was proud of her school and teachers. She believed in herself, her ideas, her teachers, and, most of all, the children. She showed the world that Dewey's ideas worked. Children at UES learned to read, write, and do arithmetic, but they learned even more. They learned about the world and its people, and—most important—they enjoyed learning! UES graduates did well in high school and became leaders in our world.

Unfortunately, some people did not believe in "progressive teaching." They believed that if children were happy at school and having fun, they were not learning. There were even people at UCLA who did not want an elementary school on the campus. Miss Seeds fought many battles to keep her school—and she was smart about it. She held classes for parents in which she explained the reasons behind everything their children did at UES. Miss Seeds built a powerful team to help her fight those battles. Her group became well known on campus and in the community, as did she, the team's leader, with her determined frown.

Miss Seeds and the UES parents convinced UCLA to build a beautiful new school, with classrooms and outdoor areas that provided children more freedom to move and work. To capture the spirit of the school Tony Rosenthal, a famous sculptor, created a statue of three animals—a llama, a reindeer, and a giraffe—to stand in the courtyard of the school. Each animal represented a continent of the earth, home to groups of people studied at the school. Each looked outward in a different direction, but all three were connected on one base. The statue reflected Miss Seeds's firm belief that all people in this world had the same human needs. Though people satisfied those needs differently in other times and places, all people were connected by their desire to live a good life.

As years passed and she grew older, the time came for Miss Seeds to retire. Her many friends held a huge celebration. Hundreds of people came to honor her and thank her for what she had accomplished for children and teachers. They created a large book of letters written by parents, friends and co-workers—all telling Miss Seeds how important she had been in their lives and how they loved and appreciated her. In addition, they gave her a special gift—a trip around the world, stopping in places she had read about but never visited.

Amid tears, Miss Seeds said, "This is the mountaintop moment of my life!"

Miss Seeds has not been forgotten, nor should she be forgotten. Through her courage, determination, and dedication, she changed the way teachers teach. Schools changed! To this day, you can find teachers who use the ideas she and her teachers developed, and you can visit the UCLA Lab School, Corinne Seeds Campus. There, you will find a portrait of her; in it, she's wearing thick glasses, a hat, and her famous frown.

UCLA LAB SCHOOL
Corinne A. Seeds Campus

Important Dates in Miss Seeds's Life

1889—Miss Seeds was born in Colorado Springs, Colorado. Her family moved to Southern California, where she attended elementary and high school.

1908 to 1910—Miss Seeds studied to become an elementary teacher.

1920 to 1921—Miss Seeds graduated from Columbia University, New York City. She earned a bachelor of science degree.

1924 to 1925—Miss Seeds returned to Columbia University for graduate study. She earned a master's degree in education.

1911 to 1924—Miss Seeds was a teacher, training teacher, and principal in schools in the Los Angeles area.

1925 to 1957—Miss Seeds was the principal of the University Elementary School, UCLA.

1928 to 1957—Miss Seeds was a professor in the Department of Education, UCLA.

1957—Miss Seeds retired.

1969—Miss Seeds died.

The Awesome Miss Seeds

Background Information

Notes to Parents and Teachers

Parents of children attending the University Elementary School were an essential part of the school's success. The name of the parent organization, the Family-School Alliance, symbolized both the role and the importance of the organization. Corinne Seeds built and maintained a strong alliance with parents by fostering mutual understanding and appreciation of the respective roles of parent and professional educator. To that end, she made a concerted and continual effort to explain to parents the philosophy, curriculum, and program of activities promoted at the school. Equally important, she invited the parents to be part of the educational enterprise as resource specialists, spokespersons, and representatives to the broader community.

What Was the Underlying Philosophy of the School?

Today, few public schools discuss the philosophic basis of a school's program, but Corinne Seeds articulated her philosophy of education loud and clear. To her, the purpose of schooling was to develop competent, democratic citizens. This was done by creating a social system in the classroom built upon democratic values (i.e., belief in the inherent value of the individual and a devotion to the common good). Classroom discipline consisted of evaluating individual behavior *rationally*, with respect to those values. The teacher had the responsibility to guide the children so as to have a classroom atmosphere that not only nurtured the learners but also stimulated their continual personal growth as responsible and competent human beings.

How Was the Curriculum Selected and Designed?

The curriculum at UES focused on people and their communities—current as well as historic. It essentially was a social studies-based curriculum, with other elementary-school subjects (mathematics, science, art, history, geography, reading, and writing) integrated into a larger unit of study. Two important concepts determined the curriculum's design:

1) *Consistency with concepts evolving in the field of child psychology*

    Corinne Seeds's studies at Columbia University introduced her to the field of child growth and development. She was able to use these ideas to create age-appropriate studies that stimulated the *natural tendencies of children*. She considered these tendencies to be tools for instruction. Every study began with a stimulating classroom. It contained items and pictures designed to arouse curiosity and stimulate a child's urge to explore and ask questions. Once the study was launched, the children and teacher created a pathway through the unit—finding answers to the children's questions, building items needed to use in their play, doing art projects, and learning skills needed to advance their study. The teacher was expected to know the children's stages of development and the subject matter to be studied, so as to prepare a flexible series of possible activities *before* the children arrived at the classroom.

2) *Worthiness of the culture/area to be studied*

    To be included in the school's curriculum, the study had to bring children in contact with civilization's finest ideas, values, and accomplishments. In

Corinne Seeds's view, valuable human experience occurred throughout the world and throughout history. Therefore, the curriculum was *global* in nature. It encompassed studies of people in Africa, China, and Asia, as well as Native Americans and ancient civilizations. Studies were designed to develop a worldview and an appreciation of the multicultural nature of our world. It was expected that children would learn those valuable ways of behaving that allowed cultures to survive and prosper (e.g., creative and artistic achievement, cooperation, scientific discovery, conservation, and preservation of the environment).

How Was the School's Program Unique?

Corinne Seeds's thirty-two-year tenure, as both professor of education at UCLA and principal of the University Elementary School, allowed a continuity of practice not found in other experiments in progressive education. She and her staff developed specific structures for different types of pupil activities, today called *strategies*. The most distinguishing pupil activities were dramatic play, construction, rhythms, and problem solving.

Dramatic play was an unscripted but planned activity that capitalized on children's natural tendency to play. As a learning tool, it provided the opportunity for children to use their understandings about the people or culture being studied (e.g., how a commercial harbor worked, including the roles and responsibilities, or the social structure of colonial life in America). Each play was evaluated by the children and teacher and gave rise to further questions and research. As the study progressed, the play became more realistic, based upon increased knowledge, understanding, and skill.

Construction of items needed for dramatic play not only provided authenticity to the play but also stimulated such skills as observation, mathematics, and creativity in using the materials. Boys and girls were not restricted to traditional gender roles but worked side by side using tools, cooking, sewing, etc.

Rhythms or body movement was another way to express a concept or idea. Children were asked to analyze or deconstruct, for example, a bullfight or the workings of a cotton gin or printing press and then recreate the idea through movement (without using words). Musical accompaniment followed the children's movements, which approached modern dance, though it was much more fluid.

Problem solving was practiced, beginning in kindergarten. It followed a general pattern of (1) identifying a problem or need; (2) suggesting a solution or hypothesis; (3) trying out methods to solve the problem or satisfy the need; and (4) selecting a workable solution until a better one was devised. In this manner, Corinne Seeds believed children learned to respond to problems in a critical, scientific manner. This pattern of behavior was meant to guide the individual through difficulties encountered in life.

The broad, humanistic curriculum and wide variety of teaching strategies provided opportunities for children with varying abilities, including mild disabilities, to participate in group activities. Corinne Seeds, herself a product of the public schools' "regular" programs, practiced inclusion at her school before the term became widely used.

Questions for today's parents and teachers to consider

What parts of Corinne Seeds's philosophy and teaching methods are used in elementary schools today?

Considering the advances in technology, how might the basic premises of Corinne Seeds's program of education be implemented today?

How does Corinne Seeds's story differ from current educational reform movements?

About the Authors

Dolores Escobar and Sandra Radoff enjoyed a personal and professional association with Corinne Seeds over many years. They completed their formal education at UCLA under Miss Seeds's direction. Later, both became demonstration and training teachers at the University Elementary School, where Corinne Seeds continued to guide their instructional practice. Though each raised a family, both remained engaged professionals throughout their lives.

Ms. Radoff earned a master's degree in education and has been involved in education on all levels, from kindergarten through university. An accomplished teacher, she served as a curriculum consultant to both private and public universities. As an administrator in a large private elementary and middle school, she has seen the success of the hands-on teaching methods advocated by Corinne Seeds.

Continuing to live close to UCLA with her family of children and grandchildren, Ms. Radoff has seen many new methods of teaching. Her perspective as educator and parent has enabled her to appreciate the outstanding benefits that Miss Seeds's methods hold for children and teachers.

Dr. Escobar completed her doctoral work as a Corinne Seeds Fellow at UCLA. Her dissertation documented the extent to which the Seeds's philosophy and methods were implemented at the University Elementary School. This research entailed hours of taped interviews with Corinne Seeds. The dissertation subsequently was published: *Social Studies Instructions at the University Elementary School* (University of California Press, 1965).

As a professor of education and later as dean of the College of Education at San Jose State University, Dr. Escobar remained deeply involved in teacher education. Publications and leadership roles focused on instruction in the social studies and language acquisition, as well as the challenges posed by cultural and linguistic diversity. Throughout her teaching and administrative work, Dr. Escobar was aware of the influence of Corinne Seeds, the mentor who taught her organizational skills and nurtured her creativity.

About the Book

The Awesome Miss Seeds is the story of a child with disabilities whose courage, determination, and vision enabled her to become a remarkable teacher and leader in education. It is the story of Corinne A. Seeds's personal challenges and eventual successes, a dramatic and inspiring story of a pioneer in progressive education who influenced the lives of thousands of elementary school children and their teachers throughout the nation. As principal of the UCLA Laboratory School for over thirty years, her leadership stands as the longest continuous demonstration of progressive education west of the Mississippi. Her influence can be seen in creative programs for school children today. Her personal story, however, has not been told outside of a select circle of colleagues, students, and friends.

This book is of particular significance for children with special needs who encounter obstacles while pursuing their dreams. Virtually deaf and having extremely poor eyesight, Corinne A. Seeds grew up in an era before modern technology was perfected to assist her and without special-education programs—as we know them today—to help her succeed. Yet her self-assurance, singleness of purpose, and extraordinary intelligence led her to accomplish what few of us will do in our lifetimes.

The Awesome Miss Seeds can be enjoyed by children with a fourth-grade reading ability or as a story read by a teacher or parent. A brief background section for adults is included. The book is intended to inform today's educators, parents, and the general public of the profound effect this extraordinary woman, relatively unknown, has had on elementary education. *The Awesome Miss Seeds* is particularly relevant to the many children whose school experiences were changed forever because of the dedication and accomplishments of Corinne A. Seeds.

Acknowledgements

We wish to recognize the following individuals for their assistance during the preparation of this book.

Shelley Brown, Director, Finance & Operations, UCLA Lab School

Julianna Jenkins, University Archives Assistant, UCLA Library

Norma Silva, Principal, Carol L. Collins Principal's Chair, UCLA Lab School

Kate Tirone, Assistant to the Administration, UCLA Lab School

Laura Weishaupt, Director of Communications, UCLA Lab School

Technical Assistance:

Holly Shepherd, Photographer and Technology Assistant

Thomas Stoiber, Computer Tech

Wanda Davis, L.A.U.S.D. Administrative Staff Aide

References for "The Awesome Miss Seeds"

For those who wish to know more about Corinne Seeds, her professed methods and basic principles of elementary education, the following references are provided:

UCLA Graduate School of Education, Special Issue, *Vol 1 No.1 (Fall 1982).* *Corinne A. Seeds, A Legacy for Today. pp.* 28

Litsinger, Dolores Escobar (1969). *A Memorial, Miss Corinne Seeds.* California Association for Supervision and Curriculum Development, The California Journal for Instructional Improvement. Vol 12, No. 2. p. 145-7

Litsinger, Dolores Escobar (1965). *Social Studies Instruction at the University Elementary School, UCLA.* University of California Press. pp.215

Nunis, Doyce (1963). *Oral Interviews with Corinne A. Seeds.* UCLA Library, Special Collections.

The sculpture depicted on the back cover was created by Tony Rosenthal. It is entitled "One World."

CPSIA information can be obtained
at www.ICGtesting.com
Printed in the USA
LVOW05*2306150317
527392LV00016B/40/P